# Voices, Visions, And Apparitions
## The Angels & Saints

## The Lives Of The Saints
(Volume 3)

### By
### Michael Freze, S.F.O.

Copyright © 2016 by Michael Freze, S,F.O.
All Rights Reserved

The Scripture quotations contained herein are from the New Revised Standard Version Bible: Catholic Edition (Copyright © 1993) by the Division of Christian Education of the National Council of the Churches of Christ in the U.S.A. Used by permission. All rights reserved.

All rights reserved. With the exception of short excerpts for critical reviews, no part of this book may be reproduced in any manner whatsoever without permission in writing from the author.

# Preface
# Angelic Appearances

When the faithful talk about supernatural visions or apparitions, what is generally thought of are those visions pertaining to Jesus, Mary, or the saints. Yet to overlook the essential role that the heavenly angels have played throughout human history would be a great disservice to these creatures of God.

The angels have appeared to the faithful perhaps more times than we realize. In fact, the Scriptures tell us that Jesus Himself was given the benefit of having an angel to assist Him during His hour of trial. During His time of temptation by the devil, even Satan acknowledged this fact: "And he took him to Jerusalem, and set him on the pinnacle of the temple, and said to him, 'If you are the Son of God, throw yourself down from here; for it is written,/ "He will give his angels charge of you, to guard you"/ and/ On their hands they will bear you up, / lest you strike your foot against a stone' ' " (Lk 4:9-11).

After King Herod arrested St,. Peter and threw him in prison, it was an angel who appeared in a vision, woke Peter up, freed him from his chains, and led him out to safety (Acts 12:1-11).

For those who doubt the real presence of angels all around us, we have this statement from the Book of Hebrews: "Do not neglect to show hospitality to strangers, for thereby some have entertained angels unawares" (Heb 13:2). We even know through God's holy Word that guardian angels do exist for our daily guidance, prayers, and protection: "For he will give his angels charge of you / to guard you in all your ways" (Ps 91:11).

It should not come as a surprise to anyone who believes in supernatural experiences that angels do play an important role in our lives. The sheer number of these heavenly creatures boggles the mind: "Then I looked, and I heard around the throne and the living creatures and the elders the voices of many angels, numbering myriads of myriads and thousands of thousands" (Rv 5:11).

Again we hear from the Book of Hebrews: "But you have come to Mount Zion and to the city of the living God, the heavenly Jerusalem, and to innumerable angels in festal gathering" (Heb 12:22).

Perhaps this is convincing in itself. But do privileged souls really see an angelic creature from time to time? Aren't the angels pure, invisible spirits? This is not only possible, but it has happened time and time again throughout our history. The Bible has claimed this to be so on numerous occasions: "Jacob went on his way and the angels of God met him; and when Jacob saw them he said, 'This is God's army!'" (Gn 32:1-2); "And the angel of the Lord appeared to him [Moses] in a flame of fire out of the midst of a bush" (Ex 3:2); "Then the Lord opened the eyes of Balaam, and he saw the angel of the Lord standing in his way, with his drawn sword in his hand; and he bowed his head, and fell on his face" (Nm 22:31); "Then David spoke to the Lord when he saw the angel who was smiting the people…" (2 Sm 24:17); "Now Joshua was standing before the angel, clothed with filthy garments" (Zec 3:3); etc.

The Old and New Testament references to visible angelic appearances are so numerous that all of them could not be included here. There are many others the faithful can read about for themselves. We have ample evidence from Sacred Scripture that the angels do appear to the people of God quite frequently. But is there any evidence that they in fact speak to them? There are a number of examples from the Bible.

# Table Of Contents

Preface

Angelic Appearances

Introduction

Final Considerations

Private Vs. Public Messages

Don't Be Afraid To Explore Other Texts

How Many Of These Messages Do We Have?

Angelic Apparitions

Apparitions Of The Saints

Apparitions of Mary

Background On Medjugorje

Conscience

Conversion

Fasting

Living The Gospel

The Mass

Prayer

Religions

The Rosary

Sacred Scripture

Sacrifice

Work

Youth

About The Author

My Self-Published

Religious eBooks In Print

Educational Background

Television Appearances

Links To My YouTube Videos Concerning My National

Links To My Writing Sites

# Introduction

Voices, visions, and apparitions are internal or external supernatural signs or experiences that God gives to instruct, inspire, warn, reprove, or reward the faithful. These supernatural phenomena may also be given in order to show us a glimpse of the reality of God's nature, or to express the reality of the divine within our midst.

However, to understand these phenomena in and of themselves without consideration for the recipients of such favors would be misleading and a source of confusion fpor most believers.

Those recipients who are privileged to experience God's intervention through supernatural thoughts or acts are called seers (males) or seeresses (females). Seers are also known as visionaries when a supernatural experience involves an imaginative apparition, an intellectual apparition, or a corporeal (bodily) apparition.

With this definition in mind, we can say that a seer may experience any of the following phenomena: private revelations, external or internal voices (locutions), prophecies, or various extraordinary gifts of the Holy Spirit (such as wisdom, knowledge, or understanding).

In turn, a visionary may be understood as one who experiences the following divine favors: corporeal visions, which are three-dimensional bodily images of Jesus, Mary, the angels, or saints; imaginative visions, which are supernaturally placed in the imagination of the recipient (such as dreams or the ecstatic state) in order to impart a divine truth, to warn, or to inspire; and intellectual visions, which are supernatural revelations immediately impressed upon the mind whereby one understands the meaning of a divine truth instantly without the aid of human effort or reason.

When we speak of heavenly apparitions concerning the experience of authentic visionaries, we limit the understanding of apparitions to people or spirits-Jesus, the Blessed Virgin Mary, archangels, guardian angels, the saints, or demonic spirits. If the images extend to a non-human or spiritual dimension, then we are dealing in the realm of visions. Visions that are not apparitions occur in many ways: images of heaven, hell, or purgatory; celestial visions; visions from the early Church; visions depicting specific experiences in the lives of the saints, etc. These differences are important to note, for frequently the faithful are confused when reading about such experiences separately or mingled together. Let us keep in mind that a vision per se is not an apparition, although the two are usually found together. For example, when Jesus appears to a visionary, it is usually in the context of another vision or experience: He may appear surrounded by an image of the Cross, Eucharist, or He may appear riding the white horse of the apocalypse. In these cases, it is very important that one interpret the experience in its full context, including both the apparition and the associated vision in the process. Without this overall context, a wrong or faulty interpretation may occur and lead the faithful astray.

Another factor one needs to address revolves around the associated messages or revelations found with every authentic vision or apparition. There has never been a documented case of an authentic supernatural vision or apparition occurring exclusively for the pleasure of the senses or for aesthetic considerations. All genuine visions and apparitions must be understood in line with a divine message or lesson that the image is sent to impart. In other words, these heavenly signs do not occur merely for emotional or sensational comfort; rather, a divine message or illumination of some aspect of the faith must accompany such experiences or the visions and/or apparitions may be considered a personal or diabolical illusion. God does not play tricks with our senses, nor does He act in order to amuse, startle, or impress us. One who experiences such supernatural phenomena in this way is self-concerned, hysterical, or disillusioned. Given these factors, it is easy to understand why the Church is very prudent and cautious when dealing with claims of supernatural voices, visions, and apparitions. These experiences are rare to begin with-given to privileged souls for special reasons at specific times-and must be carefully investigated before one puts faith in such occurrences.

In the event that the Church decides a particular visionary or seer is experiencing authentic phenomena, even then the belief is one based upon human faith and reason alone; only those truths revealed through Sacred Scripture or through the prophets and seers of the Apostolic era are considered to be revelations requiring divine faith.

By the close of the Apostolic era, all that is necessary for faith and salvation was revealed to the Church. Since that time, although authentic private revelations and prophecies do exist for the inspiration and edification of the faithful, nevertheless they cannot contain entirely new essentials about the living faith or about the Person of God. If authentic, the only thing recent or modern prophecies and revelations can do is inspire, instruct, or warn the faithful about a truth that has already been revealed.

This is not meant to say that a new particular fact or religious experience or understanding could not happen through an authentic visionary or seer-only the essentials and eternal truths cannot change or be newly revealed.

There is nothing contradictory about the Church's belief in divine revelation and that which is based upon human faith. We must be careful not to fall into the trap of biblical fundamentalism , thereby disallowing belief in any information that is not explicitly found in Sacred Scripture.

It is often because of biblical literalism or fundamentalism that many people refuse to believe in private supernatural experiences or teachings. Yet we only need to be reminded of the words of the Evangelist St. John himself, who once claimed that Scripture in fact does not contain all there is to know about lesser particulars of the faith: "But there are also many other things which Jesus did; were every one of them to be written, I suppose that the world itself could not contain the books that would be written" (Jn 21:25).

Fundamentalism chokes the reality of supernatural interventions in our midst. One remains blind to what one refuses to see: "If your were blind, you would have no guilt; but now that you say,'We see,' your guilt remains" (Jn 9:41).

We have a two-thousand-year tradition to fall back on. In turn, this tradition along with the teachings of Sacred Scripture is the rock which the Church is built upon. Part of that rich tradition involves the collective wisdom and experiences of thousands of saints, theologians, and mystics throughout the ages. I hope you keep an open but cautious mind when reading about or experiencing voices, visions, and apparitions. By their fruits you will come to know them! If they build up the Church, inspire people, convert others to the faith, then welcome these supernatural gifts as a sign of God's presence among us.

# Final Considerations

## Private Vs. Public Messages

**Private messages** (audible voices or impulses) are received either through **inner locutions** or as private revelations or prophecies through the apparitions of Jesus, Mary, the angels, and the saints. The revelations from Sacred Scripture and both for the benefit of the individual and the world as a whole. Thus, when speaking of messages or revelations from the Bible, we usually refer to those teachings as **public revelations**. Messages received by individual mystics, seers, or saints can be of a private nature, a message for the entire community of faith, or both.

Because they do not represent the collective Sacred Deposit of Faith found in Sacred Scripture and through the traditional teachings of the Church, these messages are to be believed only in terms of human rather than divine faith.

Private revelations can never take the place of or add anything to public revelation already given by the close of the Apostolic era; nor can authentic private revelations teach the faithful anything new about the essential truths of our faith, which are divinely revealed.

However, authentic supernatural messages do echo the words of the Gospel and reflect the true doctrines of the faith. These messages can expand or deepen our understanding of the Gospel and the teachings of the Church. Private revelations may teach us new things about many important issues concerning our faith: particular facts about the life of Jesus, Mary, or the Apostles; a new understanding about various aspects of the interior (spiritual) life; and prophecies about future things not mentioned in the Scriptures and which d not contradict those found in the Bible.

Even of a private message, teaching, warning, or revelation appears to be authentic and benefits a particular person or others, one is still free to believe or not believe any of these messages given after the Bible was completed (or by the close of the Apostolic era). It may be foolish not to believe some of these messages if they appear to be authentic and have inspired or benefited others. Yet it is not demanded one do so.

The closest the Church usually comes to endorsing private revelations is to say that she finds some of them credible and worthy of belief, whereby one may believe with moral certitude that what is taught or encouraged in these messages will bring one closer to God, to the imitation of the ways of Christ, and is consistent with the teachings of the Gospel. One chooses to believe or not believe through the dictates of one's heart, conscience, and reason

One can be careful of which messages or revelations to believe by comparing them to the teachings of Sacred Scripture and the that of the Fathers of the Church. If messages run contrary or oppose those teachings, the faithful need to use prudent judgment. However, if messages or revelations are new or unique to what we've been given as public revelation and it doesn't run contrary to the universal faith, then one is free to believe or not believe.

A good example is details about the life of Jesus, Mary, the angels, or the saints. Private revelations and messages from these visionaries and mystics may add to our knowledge about personal details that are missing from the Bible. For instance, little is said about Jesus's life until he was baptized and began his ministry. Many mystics have revealed details about these gaps from their various supernatural encounters. The non-canonical Gospels (and many of the early gnostic or deuterocanonical texts) have a great deal to say about the lives of those found in the Bible that the Scriptures don't reveal.

## Don't Be Afraid To Explore Other Texts

Although never officially included in the essential public revelations for the universal Church (the canonical texts), they can be of great value in deepening one's understanding of these people, places, and events. A good example is what we've learned since discovering the Dead Sea Scrolls and the Nag Hammadi texts. We now know so much more about the pre-Christian Jewish traditions and the early Christian era by having discovered and translated these works. Furthermore, these texts have enriched our understanding about all the books of the Old Testament and reconfirm their accuracy and authenticity. We even found books that were not known to exist until these finds were made, which greatly expanded our previous known works of many more Jewish texts (including additional books in the Old Testament era).

## How Many Of These Messages Do We Have?

How much material do we have of private messages, teachings, and revelations from the mystics and saints? An enormous amount! We have probably more text of all combined prophecies and revelations the past 2,000 years than is even found in the entire Bible! Again, they don't have to be believed; the Sacred Scriptures and the traditional teachings of the Church is enough to satisfy our faith. It would be foolish to disregard all private messages as well, for a wealth of information has expanded our knowledge and understanding of all things related to the Scriptures and the life of the Church since then.

This book is meant to give a brief overview of private messages and revelations from various mystics and privileged souls throughout the history of the Church. Examples of different seers and different topics or categories of messages will also be explored. It would be an impossible task to put together one book that attempted to cover all of these things since the early Christian era! Hopefully, this brief glimpse into the immense treasure of our what we do possess will encourage you to explore other books that contain these pearls of wisdom.

# Angelic Apparitions

**Amparo Cuevas** (Apparition: 1988)

It is claimed that this stigmatist from El Escorial, Spain, received an apparition of the Blessed Virgin and the "Angel of Divine Justice" on April 2, 1988. The Blessed Virgin told Amparo that this angel will put a protective mark on all the faithful children of God, in order to help fight the "Angel of Wickedness" and all the forces of darkness.

**Ana of the Angels** (1595-1686)

Blessed Ana, a mystic and victim soul from Arequipa in Peru, allegedly experienced a vision of Mary with a host of angels surrounding her. It is also claimed that Ana was called to suffer and pray for the poor souls in purgatory. She was frequently comforted by the angels during her times of trial.

**Anne Catherine Emmerich** (1774-1824)

Venerable Anne Catherine Emmerich was born at Flamske, near Koesfeld, Westphalia, Germany. In 1820, Anne saw a choir of angels filling the inside of a local church. She also had visions of guardian angels chasing evil spirits away from men, suggesting good thoughts, and presenting before them holy imaginations. At other times, Anne was privileged to experience apparitions of St. Michael the Archangel.In her various od the Blessed Virgin Mary, Anne frequently described the apparition surrounded by a host of heavenly angels.

**Barbara Reuss** (Apparition: 1946)

Stigmatist Barbara Reuss from Marienfried, Germany, saw an angel of God on May 25, 1946, in the company of Mary. The heavenly figure gave Barbara a devotional prayer to the Blessed Trinity. The heavenly figure called himself the "Angel of the Great Mediatrix of Graces."

**Berthe Petit** (1870-1943)

Berthe was born at Enghien, Belgium, and had her first mystical vision at the age of four when she saw the Blessed Virgin Mary. A short time later, Christ appeared to her in the Chapel of the Sisters of the Union of the Sacred Heart. It is claimed that Berthe experienced apparitions of many angels and saints. Her spiritual gifts were numerous. On December 29, 1930, our Lord gave Berthe the invisible stigmata. These wounds became visible and bled on many Fridays of the year.

**Catherine Laboure** (1806-1876)

Sister Catherine, a member of the Rue du Bac convent in Paris, France, and recipient of the vision resulting in the Miraculous Medal of the Blessed Virgin, experienced an angelic apparition in 1830 that led her to the chapel for her first meeting with the Virgin Mary.

**Father Reuss** (Apparition: 1945)

It is reported that a Jesuit named Father Reuss kept a detailed journal of his mystical experiences. One of those reports (dated 1945) explains his vision of seeing thousands of souls- day and night-falling into hell, and their guardian angels returning to heaven, saddened by not being able to help them obtain eternal life.

**Fatima, Portugal** (1916)

In 1916-less than a year before the Blessed Virgin Mary made her first appearance at Fatima-Lucia dos Santos (age nine) and her two cousins, Francisco Marto (age eight) and Jacinta Marto (age 6), saw a heavenly apparition in a field while they were tending the family sheep. A light appeared, which was followed by a vision of a young man. The apparition identified itself as the Angel of Portugal. This heavenly visitor encouraged the children to pray and to make sacrifices. The instructions were followed by these words: "The hearts of Jesus and Mary have designs of mercy on you."

**Faustina Kowalska** (1905-1938)

Faustina was blessed with numerous supernatural experiences, including her mystical journey to the depths of hell. There, it is claimed that Faustina was escorted and protected by one of the heavenly angels.

**Francis de Sales** (1567-1622)

It is claimed that St. Francis de Sales, Doctor of the Church and founder of the Visitandines (1610), once saw an angel walking by a young candidate for ordination. After the man was ordained, the angel was seen to be walking behind the new priest out of respect and reverence for his newly-formed character.

**Frances of Rome** (1384-1440)

This saint, who founded the Oblates of Mary (1414), was reportedly guided by an archangel only visible to herself for the last twenty-three years of her life.

**Garabandal** (1961-1965)

Maria Dolores, Conchita, Maria Cruz, and Jacinta were the four children who experienced various apparitions at Garabandal, Spain. These four girls reported an apparition of St. Michael the Archangel on Sunday, June 18, 1961. At first, the young seers did not seem to recognize the archangel, but they became familiar with their heavenly visitor through numerous other appearances that same year. On July 1, 1961, St. Michael revealed to the seers that the Virgin Mary would appear to them the next day as Our Lady of Mount Carmel. According to the testimony, this is what happened: When Mary appeared, the seers saw St. Michael and another angel in the same vision. On June 18, 1965, St. Michael again appeared, warning of a coming chastisement for the world if it does not repent of its sins. Michael claimed that the world was now "receiving its last warnings." All-in-all, it is claimed that the children had more than twenty-three hundred apparitions from the Blessed Virgin Mary and Michael the Archangel.

**Gemma Galgani** (1878-1903)

St. Gemma was born in Tuscany, Italy. In the very early years of her life, she was favored with intimate communications from our Lord. On Jun 8, 1899, Gemma received the sacred stigmata. In her later years, Gemma had daily communications with her guardian angel. She was on such personal terms with him that witnesses claim she often argued with her heavenly friend. There were times when Gemma would send her guardian angel on errands for her, usually to deliver a letter or oral message to her spiritual director.

**Genesius** (d. c. 300)

St. Genesius was a famous comedian of his day, performing before large crowds in and around the city of Rome. One time, during a Christian play designed to make fun of religion and to mock the Sacrament of Baptism, Genesius was asked by an actor performing the role of a priest what he desired. He claimed, in a sarcastic manner, that he chose baptism in order "to be cleansed of his many sins." The "priest" then sprinkled water over his head. When this act was finished, Genesius saw a heavenly angel surrounded by a brilliant light. The angel held in his hands a book of all the sins of Genesius' life. Suddenly, the angel dipped the book in baptismal water, indicating that all his sins had been forgiven by the sacrifice of Jesus Christ. Instantly, Genesius was converted. Although the play was performed before the emperor as a way to poke fun at the Christian faith, Genesius could not deny hios newfound conviction any longer. In short time, Genesius was tortured and beheaded for his faith.

**Isidore the Farmer** (d. 1130)

Isidore worked for a wealthy landowner in Madrid, Spain, for most of his life. His work was a constant blend of labor and prayer. It is said that when he was frequently late for work while attending Mass, heavenly angels took up his plow and finished his job during the time he was at church. Many witnesses claimed to see the plow moving, guided by invisible hands. Others said they saw the presence of angels beside Isidore, helping him while he farmed.

**Knock, Ireland** (1879)

During this silent appearance of the Blessed Virgin Mary, Jesus, and St. Joseph, several Irish seers claimed to have seen angels hovering over the entire host of heavenly figures who appeared at Knock.

**Mamma Rosa** (Apparition: 1968)

Mamma Rosa allegedly experienced an apparition of St. Michael the Archangel on January 5, 1968. In that vision, St. Michael told her to pray the Rosary while he fought using his sword to help save sinners from damnation.

**Miguel Poblete** (1983-present)

This living stigmatist from Penablanca near Valparaiso in Chile has allegedly had apparitions since June 12, 1983, of Mary and St. Michael the Archangel. It is said that St. Michael has given Miguel Holy Communion during his mystical state.

**Mont-St. Michel** (709)

It is claimed that Michael the Archangel appeared at Mont-St. Michel near Avranches, France, in 709.

**Padre Pio of Pietrelcina** (1887-1968)

Padre Pio bore the sacred stigmata longer than anyone in history: fifty years, from 1918 until his death. In his correspondence between two of his spiritual directors-Padre Agostino Daniele and Padre Benedetto Nardella-we have a record of Padre Pio's mystical experiences that include many voices, visions, and apparitions. In one letter to Padre Agostino, dated September 20, 1912, we hear these words: "The heavenly beings continue to visit me and to give me a foretaste of the rapture of the blessed. And while the mission of our guardian angels is a great one, my own angel's mission is certainly greater, since he has the additional task of teaching me other languages" (**Padre Pio of Pietrelcina: Letters, Volume I**).

We also have an account by a Mr. J. Kelly from the United States, who claimed to have seen a number of angels in the sky over Our Lady of Grace Friary immediately after Padre Pio's death. This vision occurred about 3:00 A.M. on September 23, 1968. Other witnesses claimed to have seen the angels as well: One was hovering over the hospital nearby, one over the church itself, and smaller angels were seen everywhere in the vicinity.

Padre Pio once told one of his spiritual daughters, Raffaelina Cerase, the following: "At the moment of your death your soul will see this angel, so good, who accompanied you through life and was so liberal in maternal care…"

It is reported that Padre Pio was on such intimate terms with his guardian angel that he often scolded him for not doing his duties. One time Padre Agostino overheard Padre Pio talking to his guardian angel during a state of ecstasy. These were the words that Padre Agostino recorded: "My Jesus, why do you seem so very young this morning? You have become so small. My guardian angel, do you see Jesus? Well, then, bow to him! That is not enough…Kiss his wounds…Fine…Good!…Angel of mine…Well done, little child…Now, now he becomes serious…he pouts…what am I to call you? What is your name?…But you understand, angel of mine, forgive me, you understand…Bless Jesus for me…"

(December, 1911).

In another example from **Padre Pio of Pietrelcina: Letters, Volume I**, Padre Pio wrote to his spiritual director, Father Agostino, after appealing to his guardian angel for companionship after a bout with the evil spirit: ":I turned to my guardian angel and, after he had kept me waiting a while, there he was, hovering close to me, singing hymns to the Divine Majesty in his angelic voice."

**Patricia of the Divine Innocence** (Apparitions: 1980s)

It is reported that Patricia, born in England, frequently experienced visions of the heavenly, including three archangels and her own guardian angel. Moreover, Patricia claimed to see the guardian angels escorting the souls from purgatory into heaven.

**Wigratzbad, Germany** (1936-1938)

It is reported from Bavaria, Germany, that during these few years many people heard a large choir of angels singing from the heavens.

# Apparitions Of The Saints

### Anna Maria Taigi (1769-1837)

Blessed Anna Maria Taigi of Siena, Italy, was favored with many mystical gifts, including visions of the future and distant things. It is reported that St. Joseph, to whom she was particularly devoted, frequently appeared to her.

### Dominic Barberi (1792-1849)

Blessed Dominic Barberi was a Passionist from Viterbo, Italy. Known for his teachings, sermons, and theological works, he appeared to the contemporary English mystic Patricia of the Divine Innocence sometime in the 1980s.

### Dominic of Silos (d. 1073)

St. Dominic Silos once appeared to Blessed Joan of Aza (d. c. 1190), the mother of the great St. Dominic, before the birth of her son. On the seventh day of a novena, Dominic Silos first appeared to Joan and declared that she would bear a son who would become a light unto the world and be a successful opponent to heresies.

### Don Bosco (1815-1888)

Born at Becchi, Piedmont, Italy, Don Bosco (St. John Bosco) was known for his work with orphaned boys. He founded the Society of St. Francis (the Salesians). It is said that Don Bosco appeared to Mamma Carmela Carabelli of Italy sometime in the late 1960s.

### Ethelbert (d. 794)

St. Ethelbert, King of the East Angles, died by decapitation. After his death, it is said that he appeared to a nobleman named Brithrid to ask that his relics be transferred to Stratusway. Obediently, Brithfrid headed out on a journey with the martyr's remains. Along the way, Ethelbert's head rolled out of the cart and restored sight to a man who had been blind for eleven years.

**Ferdinand of Portugal** (1402-1443)

Blessed Ferdinand of Portugal led an army against the Moors at Tangiers, Africa, but failed in his mission. Captured and imprisoned, Ferdinand died after six years of captivity. The day before his death, Ferdinand had told his confessor that he was visited by the Blessed Virgin Mary, St. John the Apostle, and Michael the Archangel.

**Francis of Assisi** (1182-1226)

St. Lydwine of Schiedam (1380-1433), lay stigmatist and one of the great victim souls of the Church, once claimed that various saints appeared to her, beginning in the year 1407: the Blessed Virgin Mary, St. Francis of Assisi, St. Paul, etc.

**Joan of Arc** (1412-1431)

The visionary Sandra Coleman claims to have seen St. Joan of Arc at Mount Melleray, Ireland, on August 17, 1985. In addition to this, it is reported that the Blessed Virgin Mary and the Twelve Apostles also appeared at Mount Melleray on August 19 of the same year.

**John the Apostle** (first century)

One of the four Evangelists and special Apostle to Jesus, St. John has been seen in numerous visions by many holy souls of the past. One memorable claim is that of Knock, Ireland (1879), whereby a group of young visionaries saw a silent vision of Jesus, Mary, St. Joseph, and St. John, all of which were observed as lifelike, three-dimensional characters who moved but did not speak. Today there is a chapel connected to the main church at Knock in honor of the exact location of the 1879 apparition. Replicas cast in white remain at the site for all pilgrims to see.

**Joseph** (first century)

St. Joseph, foster father of Jesus and faithful husband of the Blessed Virgin Mary, has appeared to countless privileged souls throughout the ages. Perhaps the most famous apparition of St. Joseph is that which occurred to the young seers at Knock, Ireland, in 1879. Joseph appeared along with Jesus, the Blessed Virgin, and St. John the Evangelist. This is one of the few better-known heavenly visions whereby no one in the apparition speaks a word to the visionaries. St. Joseph allegedly appeared to many other souls as well: Mamma Carmela Carabelli of Italy (1960s), Rene Paulat Lac-des-Loups at St. Francois d'Assise parish in Quebec (May 11, 1982), Patricia of the Divine Innocence from Surrey, England (1980s), etc.

**Maria Goretti** (1890-1902)

St. Maria Goretti died at the hands of Alexander Serenelli for refusing to give in to his sexual desires. Alexander was the son of her father's farmhand partner, who lived in the same house as the Gorettis. Refusing his sexual advances while alone in the home, Maria died a martyr's death by being stabbed repeatedly with a knife. For his horrible crime, Alexander received a prison sentence of thirty years. During his imprisonment, Maria Goretti appeared to Alexander in his cell. It is said that he converted to Christianity at this time, asking forgiveness of Maria's mother, and received an early release from prison. Alexander testified to Maria's sanctity during her cause of beatification. She was formally beatified on April 27, 1947, forty-five years after her martyrdom. Alexander was also present at Maria's canonization by Pope Pius XII in 1950.

**Mary Magdalene** (first century)

St. Mary Magdalene appeared to Berthe Petit (1870-1943) and to Patricia of the Divine Innocence (from England), both modern-day stigmatists.

**Padre Pio of Pietrelcina** (1887-1968)

The saintly stigmatist who bore the stigmata for fifty years was reportedly seen at the Vatican by a pilgrim and devotee in the 1980s. Confirmation of this claim is not certain. There are hundreds of written testimonies of the Padre's apparitions to many of his spiritual children the world over.

**Paul the Apostle** (first century)

The lay stigmatist and victim soul St. Lydwine of Schiedam (1380-1433) once claimed that various saints appeared to her, beginning in the year 1407: the Blessed Virgin Mary, St. Paul the Apostle, St. Francis of Assisi, etc. Lydwine also claimed to have seen the heavenly angels and the suffering Christ.

**Paul of the Cross** (1694-1775)

St. Paul of the Cross was from Ovada, Italy. A Passionist priest known for his various mystical gifts (prophecy, healing, bilocation), he was also a famous preacher. It is believed that Paul of the Cross once appeared in the 1980s to Patricia of the Divine Innocence, a modern-day mystic from England.

**Peter the Apostle** (first century)

St. Agatha (d. 251) of Sicily was thrown into prison because of her refusal to give up her virginity to the Roman governor Quintianus. Agatha, refusing the advances of the governor, was denied food and water. Quintianius had her tortured, then ordered her breasts cut off in an act of revenge. It is said that St. Peter appeared to Agatha to comfort her during these moments of agony and suffering.

## Pope Pius X (1903-1914)

It has been reported that this Holy Father appeared several times to various people at the Vatican during the reign of Pope John Paul II.

## Therese of Lisieux (d. 1897)

St. Therese, also known as "The Little Flower," has been seen by more privileged souls than perhaps any saint in the history of the Church (with the possible exceptions of St. Francis of Assisi and St. Teresa of Avila). It is also claimed that she appeared to such people as Mother Elena Aiello of Calabria, Italy, and the lay stigmatist Therese Neumann of Konnersreuth, Bavaria, Germany.

# Apparitions of Mary

In the study of supernatural apparitions that have occurred to specially privileged souls throughout the history of the Church, an obvious fact becomes clear: Marian apparitions outnumber those of any other supernatural or preternatural source (including Jesus, the angels, the saints, and the evil spirit).

It may be argued that the apparitions of our Lord are more numerous than those of Mary. This may be a true fact. But are these cases as well-documented as those involving the Blessed Virgin? We can at least admit that the personal testimonies, eyewitness accounts, and the writings of the faithful concerning Marian apparitions are far greater and more detailed than that of Jesus. Why is this so?

Perhaps one of the answers to such a question involves the very nature of the Blessed Virgin, her special privileges, and her intercessory role among the faithful.

If we look at the information given to us about Mary in Sacred Scripture (as scanty as it is), her special role as Mother of the Church becomes obvious. In John's Gospel, Mary is called at the foot of the cross to be mother of the one whom Jesus loved-John the Evangelist himself: "When Jesus saw his mother, and the disciple whom he loved standing near, he said to his mother, 'Woman, behold your son!' Then he said to the disciple, 'Behold, your mother!' And from that hour the disciple took her to his own home" (Jn 19:26-27).

It is interesting to note that Jesus refers to His Mother, Mary, as "woman" twice in this Gospel-in John 19:26 and in John 2:1-4: "On the third day there was a marriage at Cana in Galilee, and the mother of Jesus was there; Jesus also was invited to the marriage, with his disciples. When the wine failed, the mother of Jesus said to him, 'They have no wine.'

And Jesus said to her, 'O woman, what have you to do with me? My hour has not yet come.'" Immediately afterward, Jesus had the disciples fill up their wine jars with water and miraculously turned them into wine (the first of Jesus' miracles in John's Gospel). It was through Mary's motherly concern for her community of faith that Jesus responded accordingly.

Although our Lord can and does appear to others from time to time, it appears that He has commissioned His Mother for the very role she has played since the wedding at Cana; likewise, He has made true the ancient promise that one day a woman would help to intercede against the forces of evil through the coming of her Son, Jesus Christ the Savior (see Gn 3:15).

One only need look at the twelfth chapter of the Book of Revelation to see the role Mary as Queen of Heaven, interceding for humanity in the fight against the powers of darkness. There, the "woman clothed with the sun, with the moon under her feet, and on her head a crown of twelve stars" (Rv 12:1) takes on the forces of Satan and defeats his aggression in union with her Son.

Although hundreds of Marian messages have appeared in the twentieth and twenty-first centuries from dozens of seers, I have chose to focus on just one example that is perhaps the best-known of them all: the apparitions and messages of the Blessed Virgin Mary at Medjugorje in what used to be the country of Yugoslavia. These messages began in 1981 and continue to the present day with at least one of the seers.

Because these Marian apparitions are still occurring as of this date, caution must be exercised until the Church has had time to officially investigate all of these appearances and messages. Although some Church leaders have condemned these visions as a fraud, many others welcome them for the positive messages of hope they bring, the conversions that have occurred, and the ongoing fruits that have manifested in millions around the world.

## Background On Medjugorje

According to reports, the Blessed Virgin Mary began appearing to seven young children in 1981 at the village called Bijakovici in the province of Western Herzegovina (in what was once the country of Yugoslavia). Within this province and village lies Medjugorje.

The seers chosen to experience these heavenly apparitions and messages were: Ivanka Ivankovic (15), Mirjana Dragicevic (16), Milka Pavlovic (13), Vicka Ivankovic (17), Ivan Dragicevic (16), Jakov Colo (10), and Marija Pavlovic (15). Ivanka received the first vision of all six seers on June 24, 1981.

Mary came announcing herself to the seers as the "Queen of Peace." Originally approved by the Bishop of Mostar at the time, Pavao Zanic, who later changed his opinion because of age-old squabbles with the local Franciscans, the authenticity of the apparitions seems to have been favored by the former Archbishop of Split, Yugoslavia, Fran Franic.

The visions were spoken of favorably by the former Pope John Paul II, Cardinal Ratzinger (who later succeeded Pope John Paul II as Pope himself), the Marian scholar Father Rene Laurentin, and the late Cardinal-elect Hans Urs von Balthasar, the famous Swiss theologian.

Over the years, millions of people have visited Medjugorje and hundreds of thousands of healings and conversions have been reported from the faithful all over the world who have journeyed to this special site. Many miracles and supernatural phenomena have occurred to the faithful when they came to Medjugorje, according to their own eye-witness testimony. Many photographs and videos have caught some of these miraculous wonders, such as the now-famous spinning of the sun. Thousands of witnesses saw these phenomena simultaneously, hundreds of different times over the years to the present day.

The messages are allegedly for the seers, the parish, and the world, with the last three "secret messages" being reportedly grave. Many have claimed that a permanent sign will be left on the "Hill of Apparitions" (Mount Podbrdo) for all the world to see after the last secrets are revealed. Apparently, the messages are similar to those given at Fatima: peace, prayer, conversion, fasting, the Mass, reconciliation, etc.

The judgement is still out on Medjugorje. From the testimony of millions, there is no doubt it has had a positive effect on a large number of the faithful, Catholic, Protestant, and non-Christian alike.

## Conscience

"Every evening make your examination of conscience" (Mary to the seers of Medjugorje, Yugoslavia, February 24, 1985).

## Conversion

"I have come to call the world to conversion for the last time" (Mary to the seers of Medjugorje, Yugoslavia, May 2, 1982).

## Fasting

"Fasting and prayer can prevent wars and natural catastrophes" (Mary to the seers of Medjugorje, Yugoslavia, July 21, 1982).

## Living The Gospel

"Read the Bible in the morning, anchor the Divine word in your heart and force yourselves to live it during the day" (Mary to the seers of Medjugorje, Yugoslavia, April 19, 1984).

## The Mass

"I wish to call you to live the Holy Mass. There are many of you who have experienced the beauty of the Holy Mass, but there are some who come unwillingly...Let every time you come to Holy Mass be joyful. With love, come and accept Holy Mass" (Mary to the seers of Medjugorje, Yugoslavia, April 3, 1986).

## Prayer

"Always pray before your work and end your work with prayer. If you do that God will bless you and your work. These days you have been praying too little and working too much. Pray therefore. In prayer you will find rest" (Mary to the seers of Medjugorje, Yugoslavia, July 5, 1984).

"Pray more these days for the conversion of sinners" (Mary to the seers of Medjugorje, Yugoslavia, August 2, 1984).

"I invite you to pray with your heart and not only through habit. Some are coming but they do not pray with their hearts" (Mary to the seers of Medjugorje, Yugoslavia, May 2, 1985).

## Religions

"All religions are similar before God. God rules over them just like a sovereign over his kingdom. To the world, all religions are not the same because people have not complied with the commandments of God. They reject and disparage them" (Mary to the seers of Medjugorje, Yugoslavia, October 1, 1981).

## The Rosary

"The rosary is not an ornament for the home, as one often times limits himself to using it. Tell everyone to pray it" (Mary to the seers of Medjugorje, Yugoslavia, March 18, 1985).

## Sacred Scripture

"Every family must pray and read the Bible" (Mary to the seers of Medjugorje, Yugoslavia, February 14, 1985).

## Sacrifice

"You are preoccupied with material things, and in the material you lose everything that God wants to give you" (Mary to the seers of Medjugorje, Yugoslavia, April 17, 1986).

## Work

"Let each of you work according to your own capacity" (Mary to the seers of Medjugorje, Yugoslavia, October 31, 1984).

## Youth

"I want to tell the young people especially to be open to the Holy Spirit because God desires to draw you to Himself" (Mary to the seers of Medjugorje, Yugoslavia, May 16, 1985).

"Let young people be an example to others, let them witness to Jesus by their lives" (Mary to the seers of Medjugorje, Yugoslavia, April 24, 1986).

## About The Author

My background as a publisher author is wide and diverse. Here is a general bibliography of my works and the television shows I have appeared on concerning some of those works:

The nationally-published books to my credit:

"**Questions And Answers: The Gospel of Matthew**"

"**Questions And Answers: The Gospel of Mark**"

"**Questions And Answers: The Gospel of Luke**"

"**Questions And Answers: The Gospel of John**"

(All published with Baker Book House of Grand Rapids, MI).

On the more scholarly side, I have written the following works:

"**They Bore The Wounds Of Christ: The Mystery Of The Sacred Stigmata**"

"**The Making Of Saints**"

"**Voices, Visions, & Apparitions**"

"**Patron Saints**"

(All published with Our Sunday Visitor of Huntington, IN).

One of my recent eBooks now in print with Amazon Kindle ("The Complete Guide To Demonology & The Spirits of Darkness") received the Imprimatur after a prior review by the former Bishop Elden Curtiss of the Diocese of Helena, Montana. Released in December 2015, it is 905 pages long

# My Self-Published
## Religious eBooks In Print

My eBooks with Amazon Kindle:

"Demonology & The Spirits of Darkness: History Of Demons" (Volume 1: 184 pages)

"Demonology & The Spirits of Darkness: The Spiritual Warfare" (Volume 2: 135 pages)

"Demonology & The Spirits of Darkness: Possession & Exorcism" (Volume 3: 127 pages)

"Demonology & The Spirits of Darkness: Dictionary of Demonology" (Volume 4: 252 pages)

"Demonology & The Spirits of Darkness: A Catholic Perspective" (Volume 5: 905 PAGES!)

"Demonology & The Spirits of Darkness: Infestation, Oppression, & Demonic Activity" (Volume 6: 130 pages)

"Demonology & The Spirits of Darkness: History Of The Occult" (Volume 7: 70 pages)

"Demonology & The Spirits of Darkness: Witchcraft & Sorcery" (Volume 8: 93 pages)

"Demonology & The Spirits of Darkness: Evil Spirits In The Bible" (Volume 9: 43 pages)

"Demonology & The Spirits of Darkness: The Exorcist" (Volume 10: 95 pages)

"Demonology & The Spirits of Darkness: Types Of Demons & Evil Spirits" (Volume 11: 89 pages)

"Demonology & The Spirits of Darkness: Temptations Of The Devil" (Volume 12: 48 pages)

"Voices, Visions, & Apparitions: Voices From Heaven" (Volume 1, 25 pages)

"Voices, Visions, & Apparitions: Heaven, Hell, & Purgatory" (Volume 2, 25 pages)

"Ghosts Poltergeists and Haunting Spirits: A Religious Perspective" (141 pages)

"The Mystery of the Sacred Stigmata: My Interviews With Padre Pio's Spiritual Advisors" (Volume 1, 25 pages)

"Voices, Visions, & Apparitions: Heaven, Hell, & Purgatory" ( 25 pages)

"Voices, Visions, & Apparitions: Voices From Heaven" ( 33 pages)

"Voices, Visions, & Apparitions: Angels & Saints"

"30 Christmas Poems To Make Your Holidays Bright!: Special Poems For The Holiday Season" (32 pages)

"300 Christmas Trivia Facts You Might Not Know!: Customs, Traditions, Celebrations" (18 pages)

I am currently writing a book called **"Angels In The Bible: The Bible Trivia Series."** This is now available as a pre-order but will be fully published by January 30, 2016. Another book is called **"Do You Really Know Jesus Christ?: Questions About The Biblical Jesus."** This book is also available as a pre-order with a publication date of February 28, 2016.

## Educational Background

A Bachelor of Arts degree in Secondary Education from the University of Montana, Missoula, Montana (1984). My major is English with minors in Religious Studies & History.

## Television Appearances

Television Appearances as a guest interviewee for my works: "The History Channel," "The Phil Donahue Show," "The Leeza Show," and "EWTN: Mother Angelica Live!" (3 times as a guest).

### Links To My YouTube Videos Concerning My National
### Television Appearances As A Guest Interviewee For My Books

https://www.youtube.com/channel/UCmrULjCTF4ljSLwynLYO3fQ

## Links To My Writing Sites

http://www.amazon.com/-/e/B001KIZJS4

https://www.facebook.com/MikeFreze.Author/

Printed in Poland
by Amazon Fulfillment
Poland Sp. z o.o., Wrocław